Success
Second Edition

by

Lord Beaverbrook

Double9 BOOKS

Success
Second Edition
by Lord Beaverbrook

ISBN: 978-93-59950-14-3

Published by

DOUBLE 9 BOOKS
2/13-B, Ansari Road
Daryaganj, New Delhi – 110002
info@double9books.com
www.double9books.com
Tel. 011-40042856

ABOUT THE AUTHOR

LORD BEAVERBROOK, 1st Baron Beaverbrook PC, ONB (25 May 1879 - 9 June 1964), who was known as "Max" to his close friends and family, was a Canadian-British newspaper publisher and politician who worked behind the scenes. He was a major figure in British politics and the media in the first half of the 20th century. The Daily Express, the most widely read newspaper in the world, gave him a lot of power. Its deeply patriotic news and opinions were popular with the conservative working class. As Winston Churchill's Minister of Aircraft Production, he was very important in getting factories to work together during the Second World War. Max Aitken was good at making money when he was young. By the time he was 30, he was a millionaire. His business goals quickly outgrew the chances in Canada, so he moved to Britain. There, he met Bonar Law and became friends with him. With Bonar Law's help, he won a place in the House of Commons in the UK general election in December 1910. Soon after, he was made a knight. During the First World War, he was in charge of the Canadian Records office in London. In 1916, he helped get rid of H. H. Asquith as prime minister.

PREFACE

The articles embodied in this small book were written during the pressure of many other affairs and without any idea that they would be published as a consistent whole. It is, therefore, certain that the critic will find in them instances of a repetition of the central idea. This fact is really a proof of a unity of conception which justifies their publication in a collected form. I set out to ask the question, "What is success in the affairs of the world—how is it attained, and how can it be enjoyed?" I have tried with all sincerity to answer the question out of my own experience. In so doing I have strayed down many avenues of inquiry, but all of them lead back to the central conception of success as some kind of temple which satisfies the mind of the ordinary practical man.

Other fields of mental satisfaction have been left entirely outside as not germane to the inquiry.

I address myself to the young men of the new age. Those who have youth also possess opportunity. There is in the British Empire to-day no bar to success which resolution cannot break. The young clerk has the key of success in his pocket, if he has the courage and the ability to turn the lock which leads to the Temple of Success. The wide world of business and finance is open to him. Any public dinner or meeting contains hundreds of men who can succeed if they will only observe the rules which govern achievement.

A career to-day is open to talent, for there is no heredity in finance, commerce, or industry. The Succession and Death Duties are wiping out those reserves by which old-fashioned banks and businesses warded off from themselves for two or three generations the result of hereditary incompetence. Ability is bound to be recognised from whatever source it springs. The struggle in finance and commerce is too intense and the battle too world-wide to prevent individual efficiency playing a bigger and a better rôle.

If I have given encouragement to a single young man to set his feet on the path which leads upwards to success, and warned him of a few of the perils which will beset him on the road, I shall feel perfectly satisfied that this book has not been written in vain.

BEAVERBROOK.

I
SUCCESS

Success—that is the royal road we all want to tread, for the echo off its flagstones sounds pleasantly in the mind. It gives to man all that the natural man desires: the opportunity of exercising his activities to the full; the sense of power; the feeling that life is a slave, not a master; the knowledge that some great industry has quickened into life under the impulse of a single brain.

To each his own particular branch of this difficult art. The artist knows one joy, the soldier another; what delights the business man leaves the politician cold. But however much each section of society abuses the ambitions or the morals of the other, all worship equally at the same shrine. No man really wants to spend his whole life as a reporter, a clerk, a subaltern, a private Member, or a curate. Downing Street is as attractive as the oak-leaves of the field-marshal; York and Canterbury as pleasant as a dominance in Lombard Street or Burlington House.

For my own part I speak of the only field of success I know—the world of ordinary affairs. And I start with a contradiction in terms. Success is a constitutional temperament bestowed on the recipient by the gods. And yet you may have all the gifts of the fairies and fail utterly. Man cannot add an inch to his stature, but by taking thought he can walk erect; all the gifts given at birth can be destroyed by a single curse.

Like all human affairs, success is partly a matter of predestination and partly of free will. You cannot make the genius, but you can either improve or destroy it, and most men and women possess the assets which can be turned into success.

But those who possess the precious gifts will have both to hoard and to expand them.

CONTENTS

What are the qualities which make for success? They are three: Judgment, Industry, and Health, and perhaps the greatest of these is judgment. These are the three pillars which hold up the fabric of success. But in using the word judgment one has said everything.

In the affairs of the world it is the supreme quality. How many men have brilliant schemes and yet are quite unable to execute them, and through their very brilliancy stumble unawares upon ruin? For round judgment there cluster many hundred qualities, like the setting round a jewel: the capacity to read the hearts of men; to draw an inexhaustible fountain of wisdom from every particle of experience in the past, and turn the current of this knowledge into the dynamic action of the future. Genius goes to the heart of a matter like an arrow from a bow, but judgment is the quality which learns from the world what the world has to teach and then goes one better. Shelley had genius, but he would not have been a success in Wall Street—though the poet showed a flash of business knowledge in refusing to lend money to Byron.

In the ultimate resort judgment is the power to assimilate knowledge and to use it. The opinions of men and the movement of markets are all so much material for the perfected instrument of the mind.

But judgment may prove a sterile capacity if it is not accompanied by industry. The mill must have grist on which to work, and it is industry which pours in the grain.

A great opportunity may be lost and an irretrievable error committed by a brief break in the lucidity of the intellect or in the train of thought. "He who would be Cæsar anywhere," says Kipling, "must know everything everywhere." Nearly everything comes to the man who is always all there.

Men are not really born either hopelessly idle, or preternaturally industrious. They may move in one direction or the other as will or circumstances dictate, but it is open to any man to work. Hogarth's industrious and idle apprentice point a moral, but they do not tell a true tale. The real trouble about industry is to apply it in the right direction—and it is therefore the servant of judgment. The true secret of industry well applied is concentration, and there are many well-known ways of learning that art—the most potent handmaiden of success. Industry can be acquired; it should never be squandered.

But health is the foundation both of judgment and industry—and therefore of success. And without health everything is difficult. Who can exercise a sound judgment if he is feeling irritable in the morning? Who can work hard if he is suffering from a perpetual feeling of malaise?

The future lies with the people who will take exercise and not too much exercise. Athleticism may be hopeless as a career, but as a drug it is invaluable. No ordinary man can hope to succeed who does not work his body in moderation. The danger of the athlete is to believe that in kicking a goal he has won the game of life. His object is no longer to be fit for work, but to be superfit for play. He sees the means and the end through an inverted telescope. The story books always tell us that the Rowing Blue finishes up as a High Court Judge.

The truth is very different. The career of sport leads only to failure, satiety, or impotence.

The hero of the playing fields becomes the dunce of the office. Other men go on playing till middle-age robs them of their physical powers. At the end the whole thing is revealed as vanity. Play tennis or golf once a day and you may be famous; play it three times a day and you will be in danger of being thought a professional—without the reward.

The pursuit of pleasure is equally ephemeral. Time and experience rob even amusement of its charm, and the night before is not worth next morning's headache. Practical success alone makes early middle-age the most pleasurable period of a man's career. What has been worked for in youth then comes to its fruition.

It is true that brains alone are not influence, and that money alone is not influence, but brains and money combined are power. And fame, the other object of ambition, is only another name for either money or power.

Never was there a moment more favourable for turning talent towards opportunity and opportunity into triumph than Great Britain now presents to the man or woman whom ambition stirs to make a success of life. The dominions of the British Empire abolished long ago the privileges which birth confers. No bar has been set there to prevent poverty rising to the heights of wealth and power, if the man were found equal to the task.

The same development has taken place in Great Britain to-day. Men are no longer born into Cabinets; the ladder of education is rapidly reaching a perfection which enables a man born in a cottage or a slum attaining the zenith of success and power.

There stand the three attributes to be attained—Judgment, Industry, and Health. Judgment can be improved, industry can be acquired, health can be attained by those who will take the trouble. These are the three pillars on which we can build the golden pinnacle of success.

II
HAPPINESS: THREE SECRETS

Near by the Temple of Success based on the three pillars of Health, Industry, and Judgment, stands another temple. Behind the curtains of its doors is concealed the secret of happiness.

There are, of course, many forms of that priceless gift. Different temperaments will interpret it differently. Various experiences will produce variations of the blessing. A man may make a failure in his affairs and yet remain happy. The spiritual and inner life is a thing apart from material success. Even a man who, like Robert Louis Stevenson, suffers from chronic ill-health can still be happy.

But we must leave out these exceptions and deal with the normal man, who lives by and for his practical work, and who desires and enjoys both success and health. Granted that he has these two possessions, must he of necessity be happy? Not so. He may have access to the first temple, but the other temple may still be forbidden him. A rampant ambition can be a torture to him. An exaggerated selfishness can make his life miserable, or an uneasy conscience may join with the sins of pride to take their revenge on his mentality. For the man who has attained success and health there are three great rules: "To do justly, and to love mercy, and to walk humbly." These are the three pillars of the Temple of Happiness.

Justice, which is another word for honesty in practice and in intention, is perhaps the easiest of the virtues for the successful man of affairs to acquire. His experience has schooled him to something more profound than the acceptance of the rather crude dictum that "Honesty is the best policy"—which is often interpreted to mean that it is a mistake to go to gaol. But real justice must go far beyond a mere fear of the law, or even a realisation that it does not pay to indulge in sharp practice in business. It must be a mental habit—a fixed intention to be fair in dealing with money or politics, a natural desire to be just and to interpret all bargains and agreements in the spirit as well as in the letter.

The idea that nearly all successful men are unscrupulous is very frequently accepted. To the man who knows, the doctrine is simply foolish.

Success is not the only or the final test of character, but it is the best rough-and-ready reckoner. The contrary view that success probably implies a moral defect springs from judging a man by the opinions of his rivals, enemies, or neighbours. The real judges of a man's character are his colleagues. If they speak well of him, there is nothing much wrong. The failure, on the other hand, can always be sure of being popular with the men who have beaten him. They give him a testimonial instead of a cheque. It would be too curious a speculation to pursue to ask whether Justice, like the other virtues, is not a form of self-interest. To answer it in the affirmative would condemn equally the doctrines of the Sermon on the Mount and the advice to do unto others what they should do unto you. But this is certain. No man can be happy if he suffers from a perpetual doubt of his own justice.

The second quality, Mercy, has been regarded as something in contrast or conflict with justice. It is not really so. Mercy resembles the prerogative of the judge to temper the law to suit individual cases. It must be of a kindred temper with justice, or it would degenerate into mere weakness or folly. A man wants to be certain of his own just inclination before he can dare to handle mercy. But the quality of mercy is, perhaps, not so common in the human heart as to require this caution. It is a quality that has to be acquired. But the man of success and affairs ought to be the last person to complain of the difficulty of acquiring it. He has in his early days felt the whip-hand too often not to sympathise with the feelings of the under-dog. And he always knows that at some time in his career he, too, may need a merciful interpretation of a financial situation. Shakespeare may not have had this in his mind when he said that mercy "blesseth him that gives and him that takes"; but he is none the less right. Those who exercise mercy lay up a store of it for themselves. Shylock had law on his side, but not justice or mercy. One is reminded of his case by the picture of certain Jews and Gentiles alike as seen playing roulette at Monte Carlo. Their losses, inevitable to any one who plays long enough, seem to sadden them. M. Blanc would be doing a real act of mercy if he would exact his toll not in cash, but in flesh. Some of the players are of a figure and temperament which would miss the pound of flesh far less than the pound sterling.

What, then, in its essence is the quality of mercy? It is something beyond the mere desire not to push an advantage too far. It is a feeling of tenderness springing out of harsh experience, as a flower springs out of a rock. It is an inner sense of gratitude for the scheme of things, finding expression in outward action, and, therefore, assuring its possessor of an abiding happiness.

The quality of Humility is by far the most difficult to attain. There is something deep down in the nature of a successful man of affairs which seems to conflict with it. His career is born in a sense of struggle and courage and conquest, and the very type of the effort seems to invite in the completed form a temperament of arrogance. I cannot pretend to be humble myself; all I can confess is the knowledge that in so far as I could acquire humility I should be happier. Indeed, many instances prove that success and humility are not incompatible. One of the most eminent of our politicians is by nature incurably modest. The difficulty in reconciling the two qualities lies in that "perpetual presence of self to self which, though common enough in men of great ambition and ability, never ceases to be a flaw."

But there is certainly one form of humility which all successful men ought to be able to practise. They can avoid a fatal tendency to look down on and despise the younger men who are planting their feet in their own footsteps. The established arrogance which refuses credit or opportunity to rising talent is unpardonable. A man who gives way to what is really simply a form of jealousy cannot hope to be happy, for jealousy is above all others the passion which tears the heart.

The great stumbling block which prevents success embracing humility is the difficulty of distinguishing between the humble mind and the cowardly one. When does humility merge into moral cowardice and courage into arrogance? Some men in history have had this problem solved for them. Stonewall Jackson is a type of the man of supreme courage and action and judgment who was yet supremely humble—but he owed his bodily and mental qualities to nature and his humility to the intensity of his Presbyterian faith. Few men are so fortunately compounded.

Still, if the moral judgment is worth anything, a man should be able to practise courage without arrogance and to walk humbly without fear. If he can accomplish the feat he will reap no material reward, but an immense harvest of inner well-being. He will have found the blue bird of happiness which escapes so easily from the snare. He will have joined Justice to Mercy and added Humility to Courage, and in the light of this self-knowledge he will have attained the zenith of a perpetual satisfaction.

III
LUCK

Some of the critics do not believe that the pinnacle of success stands only on the three pillars of Judgment, Industry, and Health. They point out that I have omitted one vital factor—Luck. So widespread is this belief, largely pagan in its origin, that mere fortune either makes or unmakes men, that it seems worth while to discuss and refute this dangerous delusion.

Of course, if the doctrine merely means that men are the victims of circumstances and surroundings, it is a truism. It is luckier to be born heir to a peerage and £100,000 than to be born in Whitechapel. Past and present Chancellors of the Exchequer have gone far in removing much of this discrepancy in fortune. Again, a disaster which destroys a single individual may alter the whole course of a survivor's career. But the devotees of the Goddess of Luck do not mean this at all. They hold that some men are born lucky and others unlucky, as though some Fortune presided at their birth; and that, irrespective of all merits, success goes to those on whom Fortune smiles and defeat to those on whom she frowns. Or at least luck is regarded as a kind of attribute of a man like a capacity for arithmetic or games.

This view is in essence the belief of the true gambler—not the man who backs his skill at cards, or his knowledge of racing against his rival—but who goes to the tables at Monte Carlo backing runs of good or ill luck. It has been defined as a belief in the imagined tendencies of chance to produce events continuously favourable or continuously unfavourable.

The whole conception is a nightmare of the mind, peculiarly unfavourable to success in business. The laws of games of chance are as inexorable as those of the universe. A skilful player will, in the long run, defeat a less skilful one; the bank at Monte Carlo will always beat the individual if he stays long enough. I presume that the bank there is managed honestly, although I neither know nor care whether it is. But this at least is certain—the cagnotte gains 3 per cent. on every spin. Mathematically, a man is bound to lose the capital he invests in every thirty throws when his luck is neither good nor bad. In the long run his luck will leave him with a balanced book—minus the cagnotte. My advice to any man would be, "Never play roulette at all; but if you must play, hold the cagnotte."

The Press, of course, often publishes stories of great fortunes made at Monte Carlo. The proprietors there understand publicity. Such statements bring them new patrons.

It is necessary to dwell on this gambling side of the question, because every man who believes in luck has a touch of the gambler in him, though he may never have played a stake. And from the point of view of real success in affairs the gambler is doomed in advance. It is a frame of mind which a man should discourage severely when he finds it within the citadel of his mind. It is a view which too frequently infects young men with more ambition than industry.

The view of Fortune as some shining goddess sweeping down from heaven and touching the lucky recipient with her pinions of gold dazzles the mind of youth. Men think that with a single stroke they will either be made rich for life or impoverished for ever.

The more usual view is less ambitious. It is the complaint that Fortune has never looked a man's way. Failure due to lack of industry is excused on the ground that the goddess has proved adverse. There is a third form of this mental disease. A young man spoke to me in Monte Carlo the other day, and said, "I could do anything if only I had the chance, but that chance never comes my way." On that same evening I saw the aspirant throwing away whatever chance he may have had at the tables.

A similar type of character is to be found in the young man who consistently refuses good offers or even small chances of work because they are not good enough for him. He expects that Luck will suddenly bestow on him a ready-made position or a gorgeous chance suitable to the high opinions he holds of his own capacities. After a time people tire of giving him any openings at all. In wooing the Goddess of Luck he has neglected the Goddess of Opportunity.

These men in middle age fall into a well-known class. They can be seen haunting the Temple, and explaining to their more industrious and successful associates that they would have been Lord Chancellor if a big brief had ever come their way. They develop that terrible disease known as "the genius of the untried." Their case is almost as pitiful or ludicrous as that of the man of very moderate abilities whom drink or some other vice has rendered quite incapable. There will still be found men to whisper to each other as he passes, "Ah, if Brown didn't drink, he might do anything."

Far different will be the mental standpoint of the man who really means to succeed. He will banish the idea of luck from his mind. He will accept every opportunity, however small it may appear, which seems to lead to the possibility of greater things. He will not wait on luck to open the portals to fortune. He will seize opportunity by the forelock and develop its chances by his industry. Here and there he may go wrong, where judgment or experience is lacking. But out of his very defeats he will learn to do better in the future, and in the maturity of his knowledge he will attain success. At least, he will not be found sitting down and whining that luck alone has been against him.

There remains a far more subtle argument in favour of the gambling temperament which believes in luck. It is that certain men possess a kind of sixth sense in the realm of speculative enterprise. These men, it is said, know by inherent instinct, divorced from reasoned knowledge, what enterprise will succeed or fail, or whether the market will rise or fall. They are the children of fortune.

The real diagnosis of these cases is a very different one from that put forward by the mystic apostles of the Golden Luck. Eminent men who are closely in touch with the great affairs of politics or business often act on what appears to be a mere instinct of this kind. But, in truth, they have absorbed, through a careful and continuous study of events both in the present and the past, so much knowledge, that their minds reach a conclusion automatically, just as the heart beats without any stimulus from the brain. Ask them for the reasons of their decision, and they become inarticulate or unintelligible in their replies. Their conscious mind cannot explain the long-hoarded experience of their subconscious self. When they prove right in their forecast, the world exclaims, "What luck!" Well, if luck of that kind is long enough continued it will be best ascribed to judgment.

The real "lucky" speculator is of a very different character. He makes a brilliant coup or so and then disappears in some overwhelming disaster. He is as quick in losing his fortune as he is in making it. Nothing except Judgment and Industry, backed by Health, will ensure real and permanent success. The rest is sheer superstition.

Two pictures may be put before the believer in luck as an element in success. The one is Monte Carlo—where the Goddess Fortune is chiefly worshipped—steeped in almost perpetual sunshine, piled in castellated masses against its hills, gaining the sense of the illimitable from the blue horizon of the Mediterranean—a shining land meant for clean exercise and repose. Yet there youth is only seen in its depravity, while old age flocks to the central gambling hell to excite or mortify its jaded appetites by playing a game it is bound to lose.

Here you may see in their decay the people who believe in luck, steeped in an atmosphere of smoke and excitement, while beauty of Nature or the pursuits of health call to them in vain. Three badly lighted tennis courts compete with thirty splendidly furnished casino rooms. But of means for obtaining the results of exercise without the exertion there is no end. The Salle des Bains offers to the fat and the jaded the hot bath, the electric massage, and all the mechanical instruments for restoring energy. Modern science and art combine to outdo the attractions of the baths of Imperial Rome.

In far different surroundings from these were born the careers of the living captains of modern industry and finance—Inchcape, Pirrie, Cowdray, Leverhulme, or McKenna. These men believed in industry, not in fortune, and in judgment rather than in chance. The youth of this generation will do well to be guided by their example, and follow their road to success. Not by the worship of the Goddess of Luck were the great fortunes established or the great reputations made.

It is natural and right for youth to hope, but if hope turns to a belief in luck, it becomes a poison to the mind. The youth of England has before it a splendid opportunity, but let it remember always that nothing but work and brains counts, and that a man can even work himself into brains. No goddess will open to any man the portals of the temple of success. Young men must advance boldly to the central shrine along the arduous but well-tried avenues of Judgment and Industry.

IV
MODERATION

Judgment, Industry, and Health, as the instruments of success, depend largely on a fourth quality, which may be called either restraint or moderation. The successful men of these arduous days are those who control themselves strictly.

Those who are learned in the past may point out exceptions to this rule. But Charles James Fox or Bolingbroke were only competing with equals in the art of genteel debauchery. Their habits were those of their competitors. They were not fighting men who safeguarded their health and kept a cool head in the morning. It is impossible to imagine to-day a leader of the Opposition who, after a night of gambling at faro, would go down without a breakfast or a bath to develop an important attack on the Government. The days of the brilliant debauchee are over. Politicians no longer retire for good at forty to nurse the gout. The antagonists that careless genius would have to meet in the modern world would be of sterner stuff.

The modern men of action realise that a sacrifice of health is a sacrifice of years—and that every year is of value. They protect their constitutions as the final bulwark against the assault of the enemy. A man without a digestion is likely to be a man without a heart. Political and financial courage spring as much from the nerves or the stomach as from the brain. And without courage no politician or business man is worth anything. Moderation is, therefore, the secret of success.

And, above all, I would urge on ambitious youth the absolute necessity of moderation in alcohol. I am the last man in the world to be in favour of the regulation of the social habits of the people by law. Here every man should be his own controller and law-giver. But this much is certain: no man can achieve success who is not strict with himself in this matter; nor is it a bad thing for an aspiring man of business to be a teetotaller.

Take the case of the Prime Minister. No man is more careful of himself. He sips a single glass of burgundy at dinner for the obvious reason that he enjoys it, and not because it might stimulate his activities. He has given up the use of tobacco. Bolingbroke as a master of manoeuvres would have had a poor chance against him. For Bolingbroke lost his nerve in the final disaster, whereas the Prime Minister could always be trusted to have all his wits and courage about him. Mr. Lloyd George is regarded as a man riding the storm of politics with nerves to drive him on. No view could be more untrue. In the very worst days of the war in 1916 he could be discovered at the War Office taking his ten minutes' nap with his feet up on a chair and discarded newspapers lying like the débris of a battle-field about him. It would be charitable to suppose that he had fallen asleep before he had read his newspapers! He even takes his golf in very moderate doses. We are often told that he needs a prolonged holiday, but somewhere in his youth he finds inexhaustible reserves of power which he conserves into his middle age. In this way he has found the secret of his temporary Empire. It is for this reason that the man in command is never too busy to see a caller who has the urgency of vital business at his back.

The Ex-Leader of the Conservative Party, Mr. Bonar Law, however much he may differ from the Premier in many aspects of his temperament, also finds the foundation of his judgment in exercise and caution. As a player of games he is rather poor, but makes up in enthusiasm for tennis what he lacks in skill. His habits are almost ascetic in their rigour. He drinks nothing, and the finest dinner a cook ever conceived would be wasted on him. A single course of the plainest food suffices his appetite, and he grows manifestly uneasy when faced with a long meal. His pipe, his one relaxation, never far absent, seems to draw him with a magic attraction. As it was, his physical resources stood perhaps the greatest strain that has been imposed on any public man in our time. From the moment when he joined the first Coalition Government in 1915 to the day when he laid down office in 1921 he was beset by cares and immersed in labours which would have overwhelmed almost any other man. Neither this nor succeeding Coalition Governments were popular with a great section of his Conservative followers, and to the task of taking decisions on the war was added the constant and irritating necessity of keeping his own supporters in line with the administration. In 1916 he had to take the vital decision which displaced Mr. Asquith in favour of Mr. Lloyd George, and during the latter's Premiership he had to suffer the strain of constantly accommodating himself, out of a feeling of personal loyalty, to methods which were not congenial to his own nature. In the face of all these stresses he never would take a holiday, and nothing except the rigid moderation of his life enabled him to keep the cool penetration of his judgment intact and his physical vigour going during those six terrible years.

The Lord Chancellor might appear to be an exception to the rule. This is very far from being the case. It is true that his temperament knows no mean either in work or play. One of the most successful speeches he ever delivered in the House of Commons was the fruit of a day of violent exercise, followed by a night of preparation, with a wet towel tied round the head. And yet he appeared perfectly fresh; he has the priceless asset of the most marvellous constitution in the British Empire. Kipling's poem on France suggests an adaptation to describe the Lord Chancellor:

> "Furious in luxury, merciless in toil,
> Terrible with strength renewed from a tireless soil."

No man has spent himself more freely in the hunting-field or works harder to-day at games. Yet, with all this tendency to the extreme of work and play, he is a man of iron resolution and determined self-control. Although the most formidable enemy of the Pussyfooters and the most powerful protector of freedom in the social habits of the people that the Cabinet contains, he is, like Mr. Bonar Law, a teetotaler. It is this capacity for governing himself which is pointing upwards to still greater heights of power.

Mr. McKenna is, perhaps, the most striking instance of what determination can achieve in the way of health and physique. His rowing Blue was the simple and direct result of taking pains—in the form of a rowing dummy in which he practised in his own rooms. The achievement was typical of a career which has in its dual success no parallel in modern life. There have been many Chancellors of the Exchequer and many big men in the City. That a man, after forcing his way to the front in politics, should transfer his activities to the City and become in a short four years its most commanding figure is unheard of. And Mr. McKenna had the misfortune to enter public life with the handicap of a stutter. He set himself to cure it by reading Burke aloud to his family, and he cured it. He was then told by his political friends that he spoke too quickly to be effective. He cured himself of this defect too, by rehearsing his speeches to a time machine—an ordinary stop-watch, not one of the H. G. Wells' variety. Indeed, if any man can be said to have "made himself," it is Mr. McKenna. He bridges the gulf between politics and the City, and brings one to a final instance of the purely business man.

Mr. Gordon Selfridge is an exemplar of the simple life practical in the midst of unbounded success. He goes to his office every morning regularly at nine o'clock. In the midst of opulence he eats a frugal lunch in a room which supplies the one thing of which he is avaricious—big windows and plenty of fresh air. For light and air spell for him, as for the rest of us, health and sound judgment. He possesses, indeed, one terrible and hidden secret—a kind of baron's castle somewhere in the heart of South England, where he may retire beyond the pursuit of King or people, and hurl his defiance from its walls to all the intruders which threaten the balance of the mind. No one has yet discovered this castle, for it exists only on paper. When Mr. Gordon Selfridge requires mental relaxation, he may be found poring over the plans which are to be the basis of this fairy edifice. Moat and parapet, tower, dungeon, and drawbridge, are all there, only awaiting the Mason of the future to translate them into actuality. But the success of Mr. Selfridge lies in his frugality, and not in his dreams. One can afford to have a castle in Spain when one possesses the money to pay for it.

It is the complexity of modern life which enforces moderation. Science has created vast populations and huge industries, and also given the means by which single minds can direct them. Invention gives these gifts, and compels man to use them. Man is as much the slave as the master of the machine, as he turns to the telephone or the telegram. In this fierce turmoil of the modern world he can only keep his judgment intact, his nerves sound, and his mind secure by the process of self-discipline, which may be equally defined as restraint, control, or moderation. This is the price which must be paid for the gifts the gods confer.

V
MONEY

Many serious letters and a half-humorous criticism in *Punch* suggest that I am to be regarded as the apostle of a pure materialism. That is not so. I quite recognise the existence of other ambitions in the walks of Art, Religion, or Literature. But at the very outset I confined the scope of my advice to those who wish to triumph in practical affairs. I am talking to the young men who want to succeed in business and to build up a new nation. Criticism based on any other conception of my purpose is a spent shaft.

Money—the word has a magical sound. It conjures up before the vision some kind of enchanted paradise where to wish is to have—Aladdin's lamp brought down to earth.

Yet in reality money carries with it only two qualities of value: the character it creates in the making; the self-expression of the individuality in the use of it, when once it has been made. The art of making money implies all those qualities—resolution, concentration, economy, self-control—which make for success and happiness. The power of using it makes a man who has become the captain of his own soul in the process of its acquirement also the master of the circumstances which surround him. He can shape his immediate world to his own liking. Apart from these two faculties, character in acquirement, power in use, money has little value, and is just as likely to be a curse as a blessing. For this reason the money master will care little for leaving vast wealth to his descendants. He knows that they would be better men for going down stripped into the struggle, with no inheritance but that of brains and character. Wealth without either the wish, the brains, or the power to use it is too often the medium through which men pamper the flesh with good living, and the mind with inanity, until death, operating through the liver, hurries the fortunate youth into an early grave. The inheritance tax should have no terrors for the millionaire.

The value of money is, therefore, first in the striving for it and then in the use of it. The ambition itself is a fine one—but how is it to be achieved?

I would lay down certain definite rules for the guidance of the young man who, starting with small things, is determined to go on to great ones:—

1. The first key which opens the door of success is the trading instinct, the knowledge and sense of the real value of any article. Without it a man need not trouble to enter business at all, but if he possesses it even in a rudimentary form he can cultivate it in the early days when the mind is still plastic, until it develops beyond all recognition. When I was a boy I knew the value in exchange of every marble in my village, and this practice of valuing became a subconscious habit until, so long as I remained in business, I always had an intuitive perception of the real and not the face value of any article.

The young man who will walk through life developing the capacity for determining values, and then correcting his judgments by his information, is the man who will succeed in business.

2. But supposing that a young man has acquired this sense of values, he may yet ruin himself before he comes to the fruition of his talent if he will not practise economy. By economy I mean the economic conduct of his business. Examine your profit and loss account before you go out to conquer the financial world, and then go out for conquest—if the account justifies the enterprise. Too many men spend their time in laying down "pipe-lines" for future profits which may not arrive or only arrive for some newcomer who has taken over the business. There is nothing like sticking to one line of business until you have mastered it. A man who has learned how to conduct a single industry at a profit has conquered the obstacles which stand in the way of success in the larger world of enterprise.

3. Do not try to cut with too wide a swath. This last rule is the most important of all. Many promising young men have fallen into ruin from the neglect of this simple principle. It is so easy for premature ambition to launch men out into daring schemes for which they have neither the resources nor the experience. Acquire the knowledge of values, practise economy, and learn to read the minds of men, and your technique will then be perfected and ready for use on wider fields. The instinct for values, the habit of

economy, the technique of business, are only three forms of the supreme quality of that judgment which is success.

For these reasons it is the first £10,000 which counts. There is the real struggle, the test of character, and the warranty of success. Youth and strength are given us to use in that first struggle, and a man must feel those early deals right down to the pit of his stomach if he is going to be a great man of business. They must shake the very fibre of his being as the conception of a great picture shakes an artist. But the first ten thousand made, he can advance with greater freedom and take affairs in his stride. He will have the confidence of experience, and can paint with a big brush because all the details of affairs are now familiar to his mentality. With this assured technique nothing will check the career. "Why," says the innkeeper in an adaptation from Bernard Shaw's sketch of Napoleon in Italy, "conquering countries is like folding a tablecloth. Once the first fold is made, the rest is easy. Conquer one, conquer all."

Such in effect is the career of the great captains of industry. Yet the man who attains, by the practice of these rules, a great fortune, may fail of real achievement and happiness. He may not be able to recognise that the qualities of the aspirant are not exactly the qualities of the man who has arrived. The sense of general responsibility must supersede the spirit of private adventure.

The stability of credit becomes the watchword of high finance. Thus the great money master will not believe that periods of depression are of necessity ruinous. It is true that no great profits will be made in such years of depression. But the lean years will not last for ever. Industry during the period of deflation goes through a process like that of an over-fat man taking a Turkish bath. The extravagances are eliminated, new invention and energy spring up to meet the call of necessity, and when the boom years come again it finds industry, like a highly trained athlete, ready to pour out the goods and pay the wages. Economic methods are nurtured by depression.

But when all has been said and done, the sceptic may still question us. Is the capacity to make money something to be desired and striven for, something worth having in the character, some proof of ability in the mind? The answer is "Yes."

Money which is striven for brings with it the real qualities in life. Here are the counters which mark character and brains. The money brain is, in the modern world, the supreme brain. Why? Because that which the greatest number of men strive for will produce the fiercest competition of intellect. Politics are for the few; they are a game, a fancy, or an inheritance. Leaving out the man of genius who flares out, perhaps, once or twice in a century, the amount of ability which enables a man to cut a very respectable figure in a Cabinet is extraordinarily low, compared with that demanded in the world of industry and finance. The politician will never believe this, but it is so.

The battles of the market-place are real duels, on which realities of life and death and fortune or poverty and even of fame depend. Here men fight with a precipice behind them, not a pension of £2,000 a year. The young men who go down into that press must win their spurs by no man's favour. But youth can triumph; it has the resolution when the mind is still plastic to gain that judgment which experience gives.

My advice to the young men of to-day is simply this: Money is nothing but the fruit of resolution and intellect applied to the affairs of the world. To an unshakable resolution fortune will oppose no bar.

VI
EDUCATION

A great number of letters have reached me from young men who seem to think that the road to success is barred to them owing to defects in their education. To them I would send this message:

Never believe that success cannot come your way because you have not been educated in the orthodox and regular fashion.

The nineteenth century made a god of education, and its eminent men placed learning as the foremost influence in life.

I am bold enough to dissent, if by education is meant a course of study imposed from without. Indeed, such a course may be a hindrance rather than a help to a man entering on a business career. No young man on the verge of life ought to be in the least discouraged by the fact that he is not stamped with the hall mark of Oxford or Cambridge.

Possibly, indeed, he has escaped a grave danger; for if, in the impressionable period of youth, attention is given to one kind of knowledge, it may very likely be withdrawn from another. A life of sheltered study does not allow a boy to learn the hard facts of the world—and business is concerned with reality. The truth is that education is the fruit of temperament, not success the fruit of education. What a man draws into himself by his own natural volition is what counts, because it becomes a living part of himself. I will make one exception in my own case—the Shorter Catechism, which was acquired by compulsion and yet remains with me.

My own education was of a most rudimentary description. It will be difficult for the modern English mind to grasp the parish of Newcastle, New Brunswick, in the 'eighties—sparse patches of cultivation surrounded by the virgin forest and broken by the rush of an immense river. For half the year the land is in the iron grip of snow and frost, and the Miramichi is frozen right down to its estuary—so that "the rain is turned to a white dust, and the sea to a great green stone."

It was the seasons which decided my compulsory education. In the winter I attended school because it was warm inside, and in the summer I spent my time in the woods because it was warm outside.

Perhaps the most remarkable instance of what self-education can do is to be found in the achievements of Mr. J. L. Garvin. He received no formal education at all in the public school or university sense, and he began to work for his living at an early age. Yet, not only is he, perhaps, the most eminent of living journalists, but his knowledge of books is, if not more profound than that of any other man in England, certainly wider in range, for it is not limited to any country or language. By his own unaided efforts he has gained not only knowledge, but style and judgment. To listen to his talk on literature is not merely to yield oneself to the spell of the magician, but to feel that the critic has got his estimate of values right.

Reading, indeed, is the real source both of education and of style. Read what you like, not what somebody else tells you that you ought to like. That reading alone is valuable which becomes part of the reader's own mind and nature, and this can never be the case if the matter is not the result of self-selection, but forced on the student from outside.

Read anything and read everything—just as a man with a sound digestion and a good appetite eats largely and indifferently of all that is set before him. The process of selection and rejection, or, in other words, of taste, will come best and naturally to any man who has the right kind of brains in his head. Some books he will throw away; others he will read over and over again. My education owes much to Scott and Stevenson, stealthily removed from my father's library and read in the hayloft when I should have been in school.

As a partiality for the right kind of literature grows on a man he is unconsciously forming his mind and his taste and his style, and by a natural impulse and no forced growth the whole world of letters is his.

There are, of course, in addition, certain special branches of education needing teaching which are of particular value to the business life.

Foremost among these are mathematics and foreign languages. It is not suggested that a knowledge of the higher mathematics is essential to a successful career; none the less it is true that the type of mind which takes readily to mathematics is the kind which succeeds in the realm of industry and finance.

One of the things I regret is that my business career was shaped on a continent which speaks one single language for commercial purposes from the Arctic Circle to the Gulf of Mexico. Foreign languages are, therefore, a sealed book to me. But if a man can properly appraise the value of something he does not possess, I would place a knowledge of languages high in the list of acquirements making for success.

But when all is said and done, the real education is the market-place of the street. There the study of character enables the boy of judgment to develop an unholy proficiency in estimating the value of the currency of the realm.

Experiences teaches that no man ought to be downcast in setting out on the adventure of life by a lack of formal knowledge. The Lord Chancellor asked me the other day where I was going to educate one of my sons. When I replied that I had not thought about the matter, and did not care, he was unable to repress his horror.

And yet the real reasons for such indifference are deep rooted in my mind. A boy is master, and the only master, of his fortune. If he wants to succeed in literature, he will read the classics until he obtains by what he draws into himself that kind of instinct which enables him to distinguish between good work and bad, just as the expert with his eyes shut knows the difference between a good and a bad cigar. Neither may be able to give any reason, for the verdict bases on subconscious knowledge, but each will be right when he says, "Here I have written well," or "Here I have smoked badly."

The message, therefore, is one of encouragement to the young men of England who are determined to succeed in the affairs of the world, and yet have not been through the mill. The public schools turn out a type—the individual turns out himself. In the hour of action it is probable that the individual will defeat the type. Nothing is of advantage in style except reading for oneself. Nothing is of advantage in the art of learning to know a good cigar but the actual practice of smoking. Nothing is of advantage in business except going in young, liking the game, and buying one's experience.

In a word, man is the creator and not the sport of his fate. He can triumph over his upbringing and, what is more, over himself.

VII
ARROGANCE

What is arrogance? To begin with, it is the besetting sin of young men who have begun to prosper by their own exertions in the affairs of the world. It is not pride, which is a more or less just estimate of one's own power and responsibilities. It is not vanity or conceit, which consists in pluming oneself exactly on the qualities one does not possess. Arrogance is in essence something of far tougher fibre than conceit. It is the sense of ability and power run riot; the feeling that the world is an oyster, and that in opening its rough edges there is no need to care a jot for the interests or susceptibilities of others.

A young man who has surmounted his education, gone out into the world on his own account, and made some progress in business, is the ready prey of the bacillus of arrogance. He does not yet know enough of life to realise the price he will have to pay in the future for the brusqueness of his manner or the abruptness of his proceedings. He may even fancy that it is only necessary to be as rude as Napoleon to acquire all the gifts of the Emperor. This conception is altogether false, though it may be pardoned to youth in the first rush of success.

The unfortunate point is that in everyday life the older men will not in practice confer this pardon. They are annoyed by the presumption the newcomer displays, and they visit their wrath on him, not only at the time of the offence, but for years afterwards.

At the moment this attitude of criticism and hostility the masters of the field show to the aspirant may not be without its advantages if it teaches him that justice, moderation, and courtesy are qualities which still possess merits even for the rising young man. If so, we may thank Heaven even for our enemies.

The usual prophecy for curbing arrogant youth on these occasions is the sure prediction that he will come a smash. As a matter of fact, it is extraordinarily rare for a man who has conquered the initial difficulties of success in money-making, if his work is honest, to come to disaster. None the less, if the young man hears these "ancestral voices prophesying war," and shivers a little in his bed at night, he will be none the worse for the cold douche of doubt and enmity.

Indeed, so long as youth keeps its head it will be the better for the successive hurdles which obstructive age, or even middle-age, puts in its path. A few stumbles will teach it care in approaching the next jump.

The only real cure for arrogance is a check—not an absolute failure. For complete disaster is as likely to breed the arrogance of despair as supreme triumph is to breed the arrogance of invincibility. A set-back is the best cure for arrogance.

It would be a false assumption to suppose that temporary humiliations or mistakes can rid one definitely and finally of the vice I am describing. Arrogance seems too closely knit into the very fibre of early success. The firsthand experience of youth is not sufficient to effect the cure—and it may be that no years and no experience will purge the mind of this natural tendency. When Pitt publicly announced at twenty-three that he would never take anything less than Cabinet rank he was undoubtedly arrogant. He became Premier at twenty-four. But age and experience moderated his supreme haughtiness, leaving at the end a residue of pure self-confidence which enabled him to bear up against blow after blow in the effort to save the State.

Arrogance, tempered by experience and defeat, may thus produce in the end the most effective type of character. But it seems a pity that youth should suffer so much in the aftermath while it learns the necessary lessons. But will youth listen to the advice of middle-age?

For every man youth tramples on in the arrogance of his successful career a hundred enemies will spring up to dog with an implacable dislike the middle of his life. A fault of manner, a deal pressed too hard in equity, the abruptness by which the old gods are tumbled out to make room for the new—all these are treasured up against the successful newcomer. In the very heat of the strife men take no more reckon of these things than of a flesh wound in the middle of a hand-to-hand battle. It is the after recollection on the part of the vanquished that breeds the sullen resentment rankling against the arrogance of the conqueror. Years afterwards, when all these things seem to have passed away, and the very recollection of them is dim in the mind of the young man, he will suddenly be struck by an unlooked-for blow dealt from a strange or even a friendly quarter. He will stagger, as though hit from behind with a stone, and exclaim, "Why did this man hit me suddenly from the dark?" Then searching back in the chamber of his mind he will remember some long past act of arrogance—conceived of at the time merely as an exertion of legitimate power and ability—and he will realise that he is paying in maturity for the indiscretions of his youth.

He may be engaged in some scheme for the benefit of a people or a nation in which there is not the faintest trace of self-interest. He may even be anxious to keep the peace with all men in the pursuit of his aim. But he may yet be compelled to look with sorrow on the wreck of his idea and pay the default for the antagonisms of his youth. It is not, perhaps, in the nature of youth to be prudent. The game seems everything; the penalties either nil or remote. But if prudence was ever vital in the early years, it is in the avoidance of those unnecessary enmities which arrogance brings in its train.

It might be supposed that middle-age was preaching to youth on a sin it had outlived. That is not the case. Unfortunately, arrogance is not confined to any period of life. But in early age it is a tendency at once most easy to forgive and to cure. Carried into later years, with no perception of the fault, it becomes incurable. Worse than that, it usually turns its possessor into a mixture of bore and fool.

Wrapped up in the mantle of his own self-esteem, the sufferer fails to catch the drift of sentiment round him, or to put himself in touch with the opinions of others. His chair in any room is soon surrounded by vacant seats or by patient sufferers. The vice has, in fact, turned inwards, and corroded the mentality. Far better the enemies and the mistakes of youth than this final assault on the fortress of inner calm and happiness within the mind.

The arrogant man can neither be friends with others nor, what is worse still, be friends with himself. The intense concentration on self which the mental habit brings not only disturbs any rational judgment of the values of the outer world, but poisons all sanity, calm, and happiness at the very source of being. It is hard to shed arrogance. It is more difficult to be humble. It is worth while to make the attempt.

VIII
COURAGE

Courage! It sounds an easy quality to possess, bringing with it the dreams of V.C.s, and bestowing on every man worth the name the power to endure physical danger. But courage in business is a more complex affair. It presupposes a logical dilemma which can only be escaped in the field of practice.

The man who has nothing but courage easily lets this quality turn into mere stubbornness, and a crass obstinacy is as much a hindrance to business success as a moral weakness. Yet to the man who does not possess moral courage the most brilliant abilities may prove utterly useless. There is the folly of resistance and the folly of complaisance. There is the tendency towards eternal compromise and the desire for futile battle. Until the mind of youth has adjusted itself between the two extremes and formed a technique which is not so much independent of either tendency as inclusive of both, youth cannot hope for great success.

The evils which pure stubbornness brings in its train are perfectly clear. Men cling to a business indefinitely in the fond wish that a loss may yet be turned into a profit. They hope on for a better day which their intelligence tells them will never dawn. For this attitude of mind stupidity is a better word than stubbornness, and a far better word than courage. When reason and judgment bid us give up the immediate battle and start afresh on some new line, it is intellectual cowardice, not moral courage, which bids us persevere. This obstinacy is the reverse of the shield of which courage is the shining emblem—for courage in its very essence can never be divorced from judgment.

But it is easy for the character to run to the other extreme. There is a well-known type of Jewish business man who never succeeds because he is always too ready to compromise before the goal of a transaction has been attained. To such a mind the certainty of half a loaf is always better than the probability of a whole one. One merely mentions the type to accentuate the paradox. Great affairs above all things require for their successful conduct that class of mind which is eminently sensitive to the drift of events, to the characters or changing views of friends and opponents, to a careful avoidance of that rigidity of standpoint which stamps the doctrinaire or the mule. The mind of success must be receptive and plastic. It must know by the receptivity of its capacities whether it is paddling against the tide or with it.

But it is perfectly clear that this quality in the man of affairs, which is akin to the artistic temperament, may very easily degenerate into mere pliability. Never fight, always negotiate for a remnant of the profits, becomes the rule of life. At each stage in the career the primroses will beckon more attractively towards the bonfire, and the uphill path of contest look more stony and unattractive. In this process the intellect may remain unimpaired, but the moral fibre degenerates.

I once had to make a choice of this nature in the days of my youth when I was forming the Canada Cement Company. One of the concerns offered for sale to the combine was valued at far too high a price. In fact, it was obvious that only by selling it at this over-valuation could its debts be paid. The president of this overvalued concern was connected with the most powerful group of financiers that Canada has ever seen. Their smile would mean fortune to a young man, and their frown ruin to men of lesser position. The loss of including an unproductive concern at an unfair price would have been little to me personally—but it would have saddled the new amalgamated industry and the investors with a liability instead of an asset. It was certainly far easier to be pliable than to be firm. Every kind of private pressure was brought to bear on me to accede to the purchase of the property.

When this failed, all the immense engines for the formation of public opinion which were at the disposal of the opposing forces were directed against me in the form of vulgar abuse. And that attack was very cleverly directed. It made no mention of my refusal to buy a certain mill for the combine at an excessive cost to the shareholding public. On the contrary, those who had failed to induce me to break faith with the investing public appealed to that public to condemn me for forming a Trust.

I am prepared now to confess that I was bitterly hurt and injured by the injustice of these attacks. But I regret nothing. Why? Because these early violent criticisms taught me to treat ferocious onslaughts in later life with complete indifference. A certain kind of purely cynical intelligence would hold that I should have been far wiser to adopt the pliable rôle. But that innate judgment which dwells in the recesses of the mind tells me that my whole capacity for action in affairs would have been destroyed by the moral collapse of yielding to that threat. Pliability would have become a habit rather than a matter of judgment and will, for fortitude only comes by practice.

Every young man who enters business will at some time or another meet a similar crisis which will determine the bias of his career and dictate his habitual technique in negotiation.

But he may well exclaim, "How do you help me? You say that courage may be stubbornness and even stupidity—and compromise a mere form of cowardice or weakness. Where is the true courage which yet admits of compromise to be found?

It is the old question: How can firmness be combined with adaptability to circumstances? There is no answer except that the two qualities *must* be made to run concurrently in the mind. One must be responsive to the world, and yet sensible of one's own personality. It is only the special circumstance of a grave crisis which will put a young man to this crucial test of judgment. The case will have to be judged on its merits, and yet the final decision will affect the whole of his career. But one practical piece of advice can be given. Never bully, and never talk about the whip-hand—it is a word not used in big business.

The view of the intellect often turns towards compromise when the direction of the character is towards battle. Such a conflict of tendencies is most likely to lead to the wise result. The fusion of firmness with a careful weighing of the risks will best attain the real decision which is known as courage. The intellectual judgment will be balanced by the moral side. Any man who could attain this perfect balance between these two parallel sides of his mind would have attained, at a single stroke, all that is required to make him eminent in any walk of life. One regards perfection, but cannot attain it. None the less, it is out of this struggle to combine a sense of proportion with an innate hardihood that true courage is born; and courage is success.

IX
PANIC

Panic is the fear which makes great masses of men rush into the abyss without due reason. It is, in fact, a mass sentiment with which there is no reasoning. Yet at one time or another in his career every man in business will be confronted with a stampede of this character, and if he does not understand how to deal with it, he will be trampled in the mud.

The purely stubborn man will be the first to go under. He will say, and may be perfectly right in saying, that there is no real cause for anxiety. He will prepare to run slap through the storm, and refuse to reef a single financial sail. He forgets that the mere existence of panic in the minds of others is in itself as hard a factor in the situation as the real value of the properties on the market which are being stampeded. The atmosphere of the business world is a reality even when the views which produce it are wrong. To face a panic one must first of all realise the intrinsic facts, and then allow for the misreading of others. It is the plastic and ingenious mind which will best grapple with these unusual circumstances. It will invent weapons and expedients with which to face each new phase of the position. "Whenever you meet an abnormal situation," said the sage, "deal with it in an abnormal manner." That is sound advice. But a business panic is, after all, a rare phenomenon—something a man need only have to face once in a lifetime. It is the panic in the mind of the individual which is the perpetual danger. How many men are there who let this perpetual fear of financial disaster gnaw at their minds like a rat in the dark? Those who only see the mask put on in the daytime would be astonished to know the number of men who lay awake at night quaking with fear at some imagined disaster, the day of which will probably never come. These are the men who cannot keep a good heart—who lack that particular kind of courage which prevents a man becoming the prey of his own nervous imagination. They sell out good business enterprises at an absurdly low price because they have not got the nerve to hold on. Those who buy them secure the profits. One may pity the sellers, but cannot blame the buyers. Those who have the courage of their judgment are bound to win. These pessimists foresee all the possibilities and just because they foresee too much, it may be that they will spin out of the disorder of their own minds a real failure which a little calmness and courage would have avoided.

The moment a man is infected with this internal panic-fear, he ceases to be able to exercise his judgment. He is convinced, let us say, that the raw material of his industry is running short. He sees himself with contracts on hand which he will not be able to complete. Very likely there is not the remotest risk of any such shortage arising, but, in the excess of his anxiety, he buys too heavily, and at too high a price. His actions become impulsive rather than reasoned. It is true that in the perfectly balanced temperament action will follow on judgment so quickly that the two operations cannot be distinguished. Such decisions may appear to be precipitate or impulsive, but they are not really so. But the young man who has the disease of fear in his brain cells will act on an impulse which is purely irrational, because it is based on a blind terror and not on a reasoned experience.

When a man is in this state of mind, the best thing he can do is to delay his final decisions until he has really thought matters out. If he does this, the actual facts of the case may, on reflection, prove far less serious than the impulsive and diseased mind has supposed.

But it must follow that a man who can only trust his judgment to operate after a period of time must be in the second class, compared with the formed judgment which can flash into sane action in a moment. He must always be a day behind the fair—a quality fatal to real success.

How can the victim exorcise from his mind this dread of the unknown—this partly conscious and partly subconscious form of fear, "which eats the heart alway"? Nothing can throw off the grip which this acute anxiety has fixed on the brain, except a resolute effort of will and intelligence. I, myself, would give one simple recipe for the cure. When you feel inclined to be anxious about the present, think of the worst anxiety you ever had in the past. Instead of one grip on the mind, there will be two distinct grips—and the greater grip of the past will overpower the lesser one in the present. "Nothing," a man will say, "can be as bad as that crisis of old, and yet I survived it successfully. If I went through that and survived, how far less arduous and dangerous is the situation to-day?" A man can thus reason and will himself into the possession of a stout heart.

If a man can still the panic of his own heart, he will need to fear very little all the storms which may rage against him from outside. "It is the nature of tense spirits," says Lord Rosebery, "to be unduly elated and unduly depressed." A man who can conquer these extremes and turn them into common level of effort is the man who will be master in the sphere of his own soul, and, therefore, capable of controlling the vast currents which flow from outside. He may rise to that height of calmness once exhibited by Lord Leverhulme, who, when threatened with panic in his business, remarked, "Yes, of course, if the skies fall, all the larks will be killed."

Panic, therefore, whether external or internal, is an experience which tests at once the body, the mind, and the soul. The internal panic is an evil which can only be cured by a resolute application of the will and intellect to the subconscious self. The panic of a world suddenly convulsed in its markets is like a thunderstorm, sweeping from the mountains down the course of a river to where some town looks out on the bay. It comes in a moment from the wild, and passes as swiftly into the sea. It has the evanescence of a dream and yet all the force of reality. It consists of air and rain, and yet the lighter substance, driven with the force of a panic passion, can uproot the solid materials, as the tornado the tall trees and the stone dwellings of humanity, and turn the secular lives of men into desolation and despair. When it has passed, all seems calm, and only the human wreckage remains to show the power of the storm that has swept by.

To face these sudden blows which seem to come out of the void, men must have their reserves of character and mentality well in hand. The first reserve is that of intellect.

Never let mere pride or obstinacy stand in the way of bowing to the storm. Firmness of character should on these terrible occasions be turned inside out, and be formed into a plasticity of intellect which finds at once its inspiration and its courage in the adoption of novel expedients. The courage of the heart will let no expedient of the ingenuity be left untried. But both ingenuity and courage will find their real source in a health which has not yet exhausted the resources of the body. Firmness which is not obstinacy, health which is not the fad of the valetudinarian, adaptability which is not weakness, enterprise which is not rashness—these are the qualities which will preserve men in those evil days when the "blast of the terrible one is against the wall."

X
DEPRESSION

Depression is not a word which sounds cheerfully in the ears of men of affairs. But the actuality is not as bad as the term. It differs in every respect from Panic. It is not a sudden and furious gust breaking on a peaceful situation, irrational both in its onset and in its passing away, but something which can be foreseen, and ought to be foreseen, by any prudent voyager on the waters of business. The wise mariner will furl his sails before the winds blow too strong.

Nor is depression in itself a disaster. It is merely the wholesome corrective which Nature applies to the swollen periods of the world's affairs. As with trade and commerce, so with the individual.

The high-spirited man pays for his hours of elation and optimism, when every prospect seems to be open to him and the sunshine of life a thing which will last for ever, by corresponding states of reaction and gloom, when the whole universe seems to be involved in a conspiracy against his welfare. The process is a salutary if not a pleasant one—and has been applied remorsely ever since Jeshurun waxed fat and kicked.

So it is with the volume of the world's business. However well men may try to balance the trend of affairs so as to produce a normal relation between the output and the needs of humanity, the natural laws do not cease to operate in a rhythmic alternation between the high prices which stimulate production and the glut of goods which overtakes the demand of the market and breaks the price.

But this change in the sequence from boom to depression is not an unmixed evil. Prosperity spells extravagance in production. While the good times endure, there is no sufficient incentive either to economy or to invention. A concern which is selling goods at a high profit as fast as it can make them will not trouble to manage its affairs on strict economic lines. It is when the pinch begins to be felt that men will investigate with relentless zeal their whole method of production, will welcome every procedure which reduces cost, and seek for every new invention which promises an economy. Depression is the purge of business. The lean years abolish the adipose deposit of prosperity. The athlete is once more trained down fine for the battle.

Men who realise these facts will not, therefore, grumble overmuch at bad times. They will, at least, have had the sense to see that those times were bound to come, and have refused to believe that they had entered into a perpetual paradise of high prices. In this respect free will makes the individual superior to the alternations of the market. He, at least, is not compelled to be always either exalted or depressed. If he cannot be the master of the market, he is, at least, master of his own fate.

How, then, should men deal with the alternate cycles of flourishing and declining trade? There is a celebrated dictum, "Sell on arising market, buy on a falling one."

That man will be safest who will reject this time-worn theory, or will only accept it with profound modifications. The advice I tender on this subject is as applicable to Throgmorton Street as it is good for Mincing Lane. The danger of the dictum is that it commits the believer to rowing for ever against the tide.

Let us take the case of buying on a falling market. That a man should abstain from all buying transactions while the market is falling is an absurd proposition. But it is none the less true in the main that such a course is a mistaken one. The machinery of his industry must, of course, be kept in motion, or it will rust and cease to be able to move in better times. But it is unwise to embark on new enterprises and commitments when commerce, finance, and industry are all stagnant. And very frequently buying on a falling market means just this.

It is like sowing in the depths of winter seeds which would mature just as well if they were sown in March. No; it is when the tide has definitely turned that new enterprises should be undertaken. The iron frost is then broken, and the sower may go out to scatter in the spring-time seeds which will bring in their harvest. To buy before the turn is to incur the cost of carrying stocks for many unnecessary months.

The converse of the proposition is to sell on a rising market. Certainly. Sell on a rising market, but do not stop selling because the market ceases to rise. A great part of the art of business is the selling capacity and the organisation of sales, but to carry out a preordained system of selling on an abstract theory is mere folly. To cease selling just because the market is not rising at a given moment, and to wait for a better day—which may not dawn—is to burden a firm unduly with the carrying of stocks and commodities.

There is a saying in Canada, "Go, while the going is good." The phrase—an invitation to sell—finds its origin in the state of the roads. When the winter is making, the roads are hard and smooth for sleighing, and are kept so by the continual fresh falls of snow, and you can speed swiftly over the firm surface. But when the winter is breaking, the falls of snow cease, and the sleigh leaps with a crash and a bump over great gullies, tossing the traveller from side to side and dashing his head against the dashboard. These depressions are called "thank you marms," because that is the ejaculation with which the victim informs his companions that he has recovered his equanimity. The man who will never sell on a falling market is the man who will not face the "thank you marms." He will "go while the going is good," but he will not accept the corollary to the dictum, "But don't stop because going is bad." He has not the nerve to face the bump and come up smiling. Don't be afraid to sell on a falling market, or you will be afraid to sell at all until you are forced to sell at far lower prices because of the weight of stocks or commitments which must be liquidated at any cost. It is precisely in time of depression that the men of business ought to press their selling and organise their sales organisation to the utmost limit. If finance, commerce, and industry could only be persuaded to take this course in the slack times, then every action in this direction would cure the evil by lessening the duration of the bad times. Not till the surplus stocks have been unloaded will the winter pass and the summer come again in the enterprise of the world. Selling is the final cure for depression.

XI
FAILURE

The bitterest thing in life is failure, and the pity is that it is almost always the result of some avoidable error or misconception. With the rare exception of a man who is by nature a criminal or a waster, there need be no such thing as failure. Every man has a career before him, or, at worst, every man can find a niche in the social order into which he can fit himself with success.

The trouble in so many cases is that it takes time and opportunity for a man to discover in what direction his natural bent lies. He springs from a certain stock or class, and the circumstances which surround him in youth naturally dictate to him the choice of a career. In many cases it will be a method of living to which he is totally unsuited. But once he is embarked on it the clogs are about his feet, and it is hard to break away and begin all over again. And this ill-fitting of men to jobs may not even embrace so wide a divergence as that between one kind of activity and business and another. A young man may be in the right business for him, and yet in the wrong department of it. In any case, the result is the same. The employer votes him no use, or at least just passable, or second rate. Much worse, the employee knows himself that he has failed to make good, and that at the best nothing but a career of mediocrity stretches out before him. He admits a failure, and by that very act of admission he has failed. The waters of despair close above his head, and the consequence may be ruin.

Such mistakes spring from a wrong conception of the nature of the human mind. We are too apt to believe in a kind of abstraction called "general ability," which is expected to exhibit itself under any and every condition. According to this doctrine, if a man is clever at one thing or successful under one set of circumstances, he must be equally clever at everything and equally successful under all conditions. Such a view is manifestly untrue.

The mind of man is shut off into separate compartments, often capable of acting quite independently of each other. No one would dream of measuring the capacity of the individual for domestic affection by that of his power for oratory, or his spirituality by his business instinct. And what is true of the larger distinctions of the soul is also true of that particular part of the mind which is devoted to practical success. Specialised aptitude for one particular branch of activity is the exception rather than the rule. The contrary opinion may, indeed, easily lead to grave error in the judgment of men, and therefore in the management of affairs. There is no art in which either the barrister, the politician, or, for that matter, the journalist excels so much as in the rapid grasp of a logical position, the power of assimilating great masses of material against it or for it, and of putting out the results of this research again in a lucid and convincing form. Anyone listening to such an exposition would be tempted to believe that here was a man of such high general ability that he would be perfectly capable of handling in practice, and with superb ability, the affairs he has been explaining. And yet such a judgment would be wrong. The expositor would be a failure as an active agent. It would not be difficult to find the exact converse to the case. The greatest of all the editors of big London newspapers will fail entirely to appreciate a careful and logical statement of a situation when it is subjected to him. But place before him the raw material and the implements of his own profession, and his infallible instinct for news will enable him to produce a newspaper far transcending that which his more logical critic could have achieved.

Leaving aside a few strange exceptions, a musician is not a soldier, a barrister not a stockbroker, a poet not a man of business, or a politician a great organiser. Anyone who had strayed in youth to the wrong profession and failed might yet prove himself an immense success in another, and these broad distinctions at the top ramify downwards until the general truth is equally applicable to all the subdivisions of business and even to all the administrative sections of particular firms.

To take a single practical instance, there is the department of salesmanship and the department of finance. Salesmanship requires, above all, the spirit of optimism. That same spirit carried into the sphere of finance might ruin a firm. The success in one branch might therefore well be the failure in the other, and vice versa. No young man, therefore, has failed until he has succeeded.

If I had to choose one single and celebrated instance of this doctrine I should find it in the career of Lord Reading, Viceroy of India.

It may be objected that, as he is of the Jewish race and religion, his is not a fair test case by which to try the abilities and aptitudes of the young men of Great Britain. I do not accept the distinction. The powers and mental aptitudes of the Jews are exactly the same as ours, except that they come to full flower earlier. The precocity of this maturity is interpreted as a special genius for affairs—which it is not.

Lord Reading started his career on the Stock Exchange, where he failed utterly. No doubt experience would have brought him a reasonable measure of success; but it was equally clear that this was not the sphere for his preeminent abilities. He therefore broke boldly away and entered at the Bar, where his intellect secured him a reputation and an income, especially in commercial cases, which left his competitors divided between admiration and annoyance. In a single year he made £40,000. The peg had found the round hole. His eminence procured him the Attorney-Generalship. Yet with all his ability and his personal popularity he was not a real success in the House of Commons. Parliamentary warfare was not his aptitude. So he became Lord Chief Justice. His great personal character and reputation gave Lord Reading in his new position a certain reputation as a great Lord Chief. From my own limited experience I do not agree. I had to watch closely a certain case he was trying, and I did not think Lord Reading was a great judge. He failed to carry the jury with him; the final Court of Appeal ordered a new trial, which resulted in the reversal of the judgment. Such a thing might happen to any judge, but a strong one would have put a prompt end to proceedings which were obviously vexatious and entailed great cost by the delay on defendants, who had obviously been dragged improperly into the action. But his real opportunity came with his mission to the United States during the war. No ambassador had ever achieved such popularity and influence or brought back such rich sheaves with him. As a diplomatist, a man of law, and a man of business, he shone supreme. Once more, since his days at the commercial bar, he had found the real field for his talents.

From the Law Courts he has journeyed to a position of great responsibility in India. Some voices are already acclaiming the success of the new Viceroy. It will be wiser to wait until it is clear whether his versatile genius will find successful play in its new environment.

But the moral of Lord Reading's career is plain. Do not despair over initial failure. Seek a new opening more suited to your talents. Fight on in the certain hope that a career waits for every man.

XII
CONSISTENCY

Nothing is so bad as consistency. There exists no more terrible person than the man who remarks: "Well, you may say what you like, but at any rate I have been consistent." This argument is generally advanced as the palliation for some notorious failure. And this is natural For the man who is consistent must be out of touch with reality. There is no consistency in the course of events, in history, in the weather, or in the mental attitude of one's fellow-men. The consistent man means that he intends to apply a single foot-rule to all the chances and changes of the universe.

This mental standpoint must of necessity be founded on error. To adopt it is to sacrifice judgment, to cast away experience, and to treat knowledge as of no account. The man who prides himself on his consistency means that facts are nothing compared to his superior sense of intellectual virtue. But to attack consistency is quite a different thing from elevating inconsistency to the rank of an ideal. The man who was proud of being inconsistent, not from necessity but from choice, would be as much of a fool as his opposite. Life, in a word, can never be lived by a theory.

The politicians are the most prominent victims of the doctrine of consistency. They practice an art which, above all others, depends for success on opportunism—on dealing adequately with the chances and changes of circumstances and personalities. And yet the politician more than anyone else has to consider how far he dare do the right thing to-day in view of what he said yesterday. The policy of a great nation is often diverted into wrong channels by the memories of old speeches, and statesmen fear men who mole in Hansard.

Again, I do not recommend inconsistency as a good thing in itself. If a politician believes in some great general economic policy such as Free Trade or Protection, he will only be justified in changing his mind under the irresistible pressure of a change of circumstance. He will be slow, and rightly, to change his standpoint until the evidence carries absolute conviction.

In business consistency of mental attitude is a terrible vice, for a simple and obvious reason. By an inevitable process like the swaying of the solstice the business world alternates between periods of boom and periods of depression. The wheel is always revolving, fast or slow, round the full cycle of over-or under-production. It is clear that a policy which is right in one stage of the process must necessarily be wrong in the other. What would happen to a man who said, "I am consistent. I always buy," or to one who replied, "No man can charge me with lack of principle. I invariably sell"? Their stories would soon be written in the *Gazette*.

This is the most obvious instance of the perils of consistency in the world of business. But, quite apart from this, nothing but fluidity of judgment can ever lead the man of affairs to success.

I once took the chairmanship of a bank which had passed into a state of torpor threatening final decay. There was not a living fibre in it, and my task was to try to galvanise the corpse. I sought here and there and in every direction for an opening, like a boxer feeling for a weak point in his opponent's guard. My fellow directors, who had served on the board for many years, were shrewd business men, but if the bank had not lost the capacity for either accepting or creating new situations it would not have been in a state of decay. The board met once a week, and the directors gathered together before the meeting at the luncheon-table. "What surprise proposal are you going to spring on us to-day?" they used to ask me. And the mere fact that the proposal was of the nature of a surprise was almost invariably the only criticism against it. I may have been wrong in surprising my colleagues by the various projects that I put forward, but in the propositions themselves I proved right.

The criticism was really based on the doctrine of consistency fatal to all business enterprise.

Suppose an amalgamation was contemplated one day I would be a buyer of another bank, and if by next week this plan had fallen through I would be strongly in favour of selling to a bigger bank. "But you are inconsistent," said my colleagues. My answer is that what the business needed was life and movement at all costs, and that buying or selling, consistency or inconsistency were neither here nor there.

The prominent capitalist is often open to this particular charge. On Wednesday, says the adversary, he was all for this great scheme; on Friday he has forgotten all about it and has another one. This is perfectly true—but then between Wednesday and Friday the weather has changed completely. Is the barometer fickle or inconsistent because it registers an alteration of weather?

Nevertheless, the men of affairs who follow facts to success rather than consistency to failure must expect to pay the penalty. Or at least, if they are to avoid the punishment for being right they must take enormous precautions.

The principle penalty is the prompt criticism that although the successful business man plays the game with vigour, nerve, and sinew, yet he plays it according to his own rules. The truth is that there is no other way in which to play the game. Fluidity of judgment, adversely described as fickleness and inconsistency, is the essence of success.

But the criticism is damaging. There are only two ways of combating it, the wrong one and the right one. The wrong method is that of hypocrisy—claiming a consistency which does not exist. The right one is to cultivate the art of pleasing, so that inconsistency may be forgiven. Friends may thus be retained though business policies vary. This is the highest art of financial diplomacy.

Those who by some misfortune of character or upbringing are incapable of this practice must make up their minds to face the abuse which their successful practice of inconsistency will entail. They will not, if they are wise, cultivate hypocrisy, not because the practice will damage them in the esteem of their colleagues and neighbours, for, on the contrary, it will enhance their repute, but because it will damage their own self-respect. They would know that they were right in following fact and fortune, and yet would be making a public admission that they were wrong.

XIII
PREJUDICE

The most common, and, perhaps, the most serious of vices is prejudice. It is a thing imbibed with one's mother's milk, fortified by all one's youthful surroundings, and only broken through, if at all, by experience of the world and a deliberate mental effort.

Prejudice is, indeed, a vice in the most serious sense of the term. It is more damaging and corroding in its effects than most of the evil habits which are usually described by that term. It is destructive of judgment and devastating in its effect on the mentality because it is a symptom of a narrowness of outlook on the world. The man who can learn to outlive prejudice has broken through an iron ring which binds the mind. And yet we all come into the world of affairs in early youth with that ring surrounding our temples. We have subconscious prejudices even where we have no conscious ones. Family, tradition, early instruction and upbringing fasten on every man preconceptions which are hard to break.

I write out of my own experience. I was brought up as the son of a minister of the Church of Scotland, who left Edinburgh University as a young man to take up a ministry in Canada. The Presbyterian faith was, therefore, the one in which I was brought up in my boyhood, and I still feel in my inner being a prejudice, which I cannot defend in reason, against those doctrines which traverse the Westminster Confession of Faith. However much thought and experience have modified my views on religious questions, my tendency is to become the Church of Scotland militant if any other denomination challenges its views or organisation.

Such are the prepossessions which surround youth. They are formidable, whether they take the shape of religion or politics or class—and a fixed form of religious belief is probably the most operative of them all. It is quite possible that but for subconscious training of the mind inbred through the generations neither man nor society would have been able to survive. None the less, now that man has attained the stage of social reason, prejudice is rather a weakness than a strength.

The greatest prejudice in social life is that against persons—not against people known to one, for in that case it is dislike or indifference or even hatred, but against some individual not even known by sight.

A mentions B to C. "Oh!" says C. "I loathe that man." "But have you ever met him?" says A. "No, and I don't want to, but I know quite enough about him."

"But what do you know against him?"

"Well, I know that E told D, who told me, that he was black through and through, and a bad man."

A few weeks afterwards C sits next B at dinner; finds him an excellent sort of man to talk to and to do business with, and henceforward goes about chanting his praises. Thus is personal prejudice disproved by the actual fact. It is a curious freak of circumstance, not easily accounted for, that men who possess that fascination of personality which makes them firm friends and violent enemies are most liable to be adversely judged out of that lack of knowledge which is called prejudice.

There is another form of the error which is found in the business world. Men of affairs conceive quite irrational dislikes for certain types of securities or transactions. They are given, perhaps, an excellent offer, out of which they might make a considerable profit. They turn the matter down without further consideration. Their ostensible reason is that they are not accustomed to deal in that particular class of security. Their real reason for refusing is that they are the victims of their own environment, and that they have not the intellectual courage or force to break away from it even when every argument proves that it would be to their advantage to do so. Their intellects have become musclebound by habit or tradition.

The fourth and, perhaps, the most violent form of prejudice, outside the sphere of religion, may be found in politics. Men embrace certain political conceptions, and, though the whole world breaks into ruins, and is reconstructed around them, nothing will alter their original ideas. The Radical says that the Tory does not change his spots, and the Tory is convinced that a Radical is still a direct emanation of the evil one. In the middle of these conflicting antagonisms the real road to national peace, prosperity, and security is missed by those who prefer prejudice to the lessons which reality teaches. The most infamous case of all to the unbending partisan is that of a man who has so far outlived the prejudices of party as to be able to criticise one side without joining another.

The advantage of prejudice is the preservation of tradition; its disadvantage is the inability which it brings to an individual or to a nation to adapt life to the change of circumstance. It is, therefore, at once both the vice of youth and of age. Youth is prejudiced by upbringing; age is prejudiced because it cannot adapt itself to the circumstances of a changing world. But both youth and age can fight by the power of the human will against the tendencies which steep them in their own prepossessions

Youth can say: "I will forget that I was brought up to be a Scotsman and a Presbyterian, and so prejudiced against all Roman Catholics or Jews; the world is open to me, I will form my own convictions and judge men and religion on their merits." The subconscious self will still operate, but its extravagances will be checked by reason and will.

Age can say to itself: "It is true that all that has happened in the past is part of my experience, and therefore of me. I have formed certain conclusions from what I have observed, but the data on which I have formed them are constantly changing. The moment that I cease to be able to accept and pass into my own experience new factors which my past would reject as unpleasant or untrue I have become stereotyped in prejudice and the truth of actuality is no longer in me, and when touch with the world is lost the only alternative is retirement or disaster."

The more quickly youth breaks away from the prejudices of its surroundings, the more rapid will be its success. The harder that age fights against prepossessions, born of the past, which gather round to obstruct the free operation of its mind, the longer will be the period of a happy, successful, and active life.

Prejudice is a mixture of pride and egotism, and no prejudiced man, therefore, will be happy.

XIV
CALM

The last two essays have dealt with the more depressing sides of practical life—the sudden tempest which sweeps down on the business man, or the long period of depression which is the necessary prelude to the times in which optimism is justified. But it is on the note of optimism, and not of pessimism, that I would conclude, and after the storm comes the calm. What is calm to the man of experience in affairs? It is the end to which turbulent and ambitious youth should devote itself in order that it may attain to happiness in that period of middle-age which still gives to assured success its real flavour. Youth is the time of hope; old age is the time for looking back on the pleasures and achievements of the past—when success or failure may seem matters of comparative unimportance. Successful middle-age stands between the two. Its calm is not the result either of senility or failure. It represents that solid success which enables a man to adventure into fresh spheres without any perturbation. New fields call to him—Art, or Letters, or Public Service. Success is already his, and it will be his own fault if he does not achieve happiness as well.

Successful middle-age appears to me to be the ideal of practical men. I have tried to indicate the method by which it can be attained by any young man who is sufficiently resolute in his purpose. Finance, Commerce, and Industry are, under modern conditions, spheres open to the talent of any individual. The lack of education in the formal sense is no bar to advancement. Every young man has his chance. But will he practise industry, economy, and moderation, avoid arrogance and panic, and know how to face depression with a stout heart? Even if he is a genius, will he know how not to soar with duly restrained wings?

The secret of power is the method by which the fire of youth is translated into the knowledge of experience. In these essays I have suggested a short cut to that knowledge. I once had youth, and now I have experience, and I believe that youth can do anything if its desire for success is sufficiently strong to curb all other desires. I also believe that a few words of experience can teach youth how to avoid the pitfalls of finance which wait for the most audacious spirits. I write out of the conviction of my own experience.

But, above all, stands the attainment of happiness as the final form of struggle. Happiness can only be attained as the result of a prolonged effort. It is the result of material surroundings and yet a state of the inner mind. It is, therefore, in some form or another at once the consequence of achievement and a sense of calm. The flavour is achievement, but the fruit should be the assured sense of happiness.

"One or another
In money or guns may surpass his brother.
But whoever shall know,
As the long days go.
That to live is happy, has found his heaven."

It is in ignoring this doctrine of the poet that so many men go wrong. They practise the doctrines of success: they attain it, and then they lose happiness because they cannot stop. The flower is brilliant, but the fruit has a sour taste. The final crown in the career of success is to know when to retire.

"Call no man happy," says the ancient sage, "until he is dead," drawing his moral from the cruel death of a great King. I would say, call no man successful until he has left business with enough money to live the kind of life that pleases him. The man who holds on beyond this limit is laying up trouble for himself and disappointment for others.

Success in the financial world is the prerogative of young men. A man who has not succeeded in the field before middle-age comes upon him, will never succeed in the fundamental sense of the term. An honourable and prosperous career may, indeed, lie before him, but he will never reach the heights. He will just go on from year to year, making rather more or rather less money, by a toil to which only death or old age will put a term. And I have not written this book for the middle-aged, but for the young. To them my advice would be, "Succeed young, and retire as young as you can."

The fate of the successful who hold on long after they have amassed a great, or at least an adequate, fortune, is written broad across the face of financial history. The young man who has arrived has formed the habit and acquired the technique of business. The habit has become part of his being. How hard it is to give it up! His technique has become almost universally successful. If he has made £50,000 by it, why not go on and make half a million; if he has made a million, why not go on and make three? All that you have to do, says the subtle tempter, is to reproduce the process of success indefinitely. The riches and the powers of the world are to be had in increasing abundance by the mere exercise of qualities which, though they have been painfully acquired, have now become the very habit of pleasure. How dull life would seem if the process of making money was abandoned; how impossible for a man of ripe experience to fail where the mere stripling had succeeded? The temptation is subtle, but the logic is wrong. Success is not a process which can reproduce itself indefinitely in the same field. The dominant mind loses its elasticity: it fails to appreciate real values under changed conditions. Victory has become to it not so much a struggle as a habit. Then follows the decline. The judgment begins to waver or go astray out of a kind of self-worship, which makes the satisfaction of self, and not the realisation of what is possible, the dominant object in every transaction. There will be plenty of money to back this delusion for a time, and plenty of flatterers and sycophants to play up to and encourage the delusion. The history of Napoleon has not been written in vain. Here we see a first-class intellect going through this process of mental corruption, which leads from overwhelming success in early youth, to absolute disaster in middle-age. The only hope for the Napoleon of Finance is to retire before his delusions overtake him.

But what is the man who retires early from business to do? Some form of activity must fill the void. The answer to the question is to be found in a change of occupation. To some, recreation, and the pursuit of some art or science or study may bring satisfaction, but these will be the exceptions. Some kind of public service will beckon to the majority. And it is natural that this should be the case. Politics, journalism, the management of Commissions or charitable organisations, all require much the same kind of aptitudes and draw on the same kind of experiences which are acquired by the successful man of affairs. The difference is that they are not so arduous, because they are rarely a matter of life and death to any man—and certainly can never be so to a man with an assured income.

On the other hand, from the point of view of society, it is a great advantage to a nation that it should have at its disposal the services of men of this kind of capacity and experience. What public life needs above all things is the presence in it of men who have a knowledge of reality. In the eighteenth and nineteenth centuries the landowning classes supplied this kind of direction to the State as the fruit of their leisure, and, despite some narrowness and selfishness, they undoubtedly did their work well. But they were disappearing as a class before the war, and the war has practically destroyed them. Nor are the world-wide industrial, commercial, and economic problems of the twentieth century particularly suitable to their form of intellect. The policy of Great Britain of to-day ought to be founded on a knowledge both of markets and production. It is here that the retired man of affairs can help. Simply to go on making money after all personal need for it has passed is, therefore, a form of selfishness, and, in consequence, will not bring happiness, and in the ultimate calculation that life can hardly be called successful which is not happy.

My final message is one of hope to youth. Dare all, yet keep a sense of proportion. Deny yourself all, and yet do not be a prig. Hope all, without arrogance, and you will achieve all without losing the capacity for moderation. Then the Temple of Success will assuredly be open to you, and you will pass from it into the inner shrine of happiness.